Emotional intelligence 2.0

A comprehensive guide to boosting your emotional

intelligence, mastering social skills , understanding

EQ & IQ

By

Derek Warren

TABLE OF CONTENT

INTRODUCTION

At my last place of work, I noticed a trend in just two months of my stay. The boss would get really angry and unleash his anger now and again on the next unsuspecting employee. Usually, these employees had done nothing wrong.

His reaction to his own anger led him to handing out a suspension letter here and a letter of dismissal there with the result that just a few days after these employees were gone, he would regret his actions and wish he could apologize.

At that moment of anger and much later, he is controlled by his emotions. His lack of emotional control is what makes him take decisions that he later regrets in a repetitive manner. For a more self-aware person, it would appear that this was just a matter of temperament but studies have shown that it was something much deeper. A lack of hold on the emotions.

We humans have been blessed with two minds: the rational mind and the emotional mind. The rational mind is the seat of reason; the power house of thinking and the emotional mind is the seat of passion; the power house of feelings.

So while the rational mind enables logical reasoning, the emotional mind enables impulsive action based on our feelings. Feelings occur every moment. They are always present. You cannot say 'I do not feel anything now'. It is impossible to not feel.

Our actions are therefore largely influenced by our feelings whether or not we realize this. The ability to recognize these feelings and the emotions accompanying them, to identify them and to manage them appropriately is what is referred to as emotional intelligence.

However, emotional intelligence extends its scope to include the ability to identify the feelings of others and manage those feelings too so that we create a beneficial and cooperative relationship. An employee who is emotionally intelligent will therefore have an easier ride at work with the boss and his fellow workers. He will be the man everyone wants to talk to and relate with. An employer who is emotionally intelligent will likewise create a work environment that is devoid of tension and full of motivation and drive.

It becomes important therefore that we know

what emotional intelligence is all about and how to develop and enhance it in order to achieve our potential and improve our relationships. This is the crux of this book.

This book will help you understand what your emotions are, their purpose, the difference between emotional intelligence and general intelligence or intellectual ability, how to improve your relationships by just being emotionally intelligent and a bonus chapter on how to use positive intelligence to achieve your potential.

By understanding how to use your emotional intelligence skills you will be able to make better choices in your life, have better relationships, be a better spouse or parent, achieve career, business and academic success and become a generally better and more capable leader.

Organizations that imbibe emotional intelligence into their company culture will also achieve higher levels of productivity, solid clientele, impeccable customer service and increased sales or patronage. It becomes obvious then that emotional intelligence now accounts for a large aspect of success in our contemporary world.

CHAPTER ONE

EMOTIONAL INTELLIGENCE DEFINED

The importance of emotional intelligence is becoming rapidly recognized in today's world. Organizations now explore testing for emotional intelligence in the hiring and promotion process.

While general intelligence (IQ) has been loudly applauded as the necessary requirement for an individual's success in any field over several decades, the relevance of emotional intelligence is rapidly taking hold even in science.

Proponents are now of the view that as important as general intelligence is, it has been given too much accolades as it is not the sole factor for success. As a result, emotional intelligence is now being included in education, businesses and communities around the world. But how come the world never knew about this all important concept before? How come it was never talked about or emphasized?

The entire emotional intelligence revolution began while John Mayer and Peter Salovey, two psychology professors were chatting about politics and painting a house.

They came to the now generally acceptable conclusion that smart decision making required more than the intellect as they wondered why a very smart politician was acting rather dumb. The concept had however appeared before in 1985 in the doctoral thesis of Wayne Payne titled "A Study of Emotion: Developing Emotional Intelligence". Dr.

Daniel Goleman, author of Emotional Intelligence-Why It Can Matter More Than IQ popularized the concept when he published his book on the subject in 1995.

He advocated strongly that emotional intelligence mattered more than general intelligence and is a vital factor for success. If you can manage your emotions appropriately to suit the circumstance and can recognize and manage these emotions in others, you will attract relationships that you need to help you climb up the ladder in your chosen field.

Emotional Intelligence can also be referred to as Emotional Quotient (EQ) or Emotional Intelligence Quotient (EIQ). Goleman has said that it 'defines our capacity for relationship'. Individuals can therefore achieve significant levels of success by maintaining their emotional intelligence.

Understanding Emotions

Our emotions are tied to our feelings and describe the way we feel at every moment. For instance, the emotion of fear attests to a state of being afraid and the emotion of happiness attests to a state of being happy.

These emotions are controlled by the emotional mind which unlike the rational mind does not allow for thinking before action. In other words, our emotions are impulsive. They propel us to action. A person controlled by his emotional mind therefore will usually not think before acting. Our emotions enable us to make instant decisions in times of trouble and desperation therefore the fear of death for example will propel one to run before looking for the cause of alarm. Emotions have been handed to us by nature to help us go through life and their overall significance places them in as much an important place as reason in our lives.

The most recurrent emotions include love, fear, anger, happiness, guilt, surprise, disgust, anxiety and sadness. The emotion of love is so strong that it erodes all reason and makes sexual union as well as parental sacrifice possible. A parent faced with the possible death of a child would therefore choose to sacrifice his own life for that of the child.

This act of sacrifice is never calculated but is rather impulsive. The parent sees it as the reasonable thing to do because he or she acts from a place of the emotions.

The emotional mind through our feelings equips us for situations too difficult for the rational mind to handle alone. This is why it is often said that passion overpowers reason. This is why falling in love recounts to us a process of making decisions from the heart rather than from the head. The emotion of love enables us to make our choice of a spouse from the place of passion, of our emotions, of our feelings rather than thinking about it or reasoning out the process of loving them.

The emotional mind however acts from the place of learned pattern. It brings to us at our impulsive moments solutions from prior similar situations that had worked perfectly. The emotion of fear comes strongly to push us to flee or attack without thinking about it because these have proven to be the regular, recurrent and successful options at such moments of danger.

A person who sees a snake will therefore run away from it before thinking about the situation. His emotions know that running is the best thing to do. They know that running is the action that has worked over time and that will work now. This is why it is possible to school the emotions. It is totally possible to become emotionally intelligent.

What is Emotional Intelligence?

There are a plethora of definitions for emotional intelligence but a unity of meaning in these definitions. The thoughts of these proponents all point to the fact that our emotions propel our behavior which in turn impacts others positively or negatively and emotional intelligence is the ability to organize these emotions such that they yield the desirable actions only.

Thus, emotional intelligence comes in handy when we are under pressure and keeps us from cursing everyone around us because we are angry. We feel the emotion of anger, we recognize and identify it as anger but we do not perform its resultant action.

We stop to examine the emotion and discard it because of its dire consequences. If we are emotionally unintelligent however, we would have acted before thinking about our actions. We would have cursed that man or hit that lady before we said to ourselves, 'I shouldn't have done that.' When we have understood our emotions so well, we would then be able to recognize them in others and influence their actions. Having said that, we would now look at the definition of emotional intelligence.

A very self-explanatory definition of emotional intelligence has been given by the Institute of Health and Human Potential as 'the ability to recognize, understand and manage our own emotions and to recognize, understand and influence the emotions of others'.

Another definition I will like to reproduce here is that given by Wikipedia to the effect that 'emotional intelligence is the capability of individuals to recognize their own emotions and those of others, discern between different feelings and label them appropriately, use emotional information to guide thinking and behavior, and manage and/or adjust emotions to adapt to environments or achieve one's goals'.

We would now provide our own definition and a working definition for the purpose of this book.

Emotional intelligence is the ability of an individual to understand and manage his emotions as well as those of others. By being able to manage the emotions of others properly, an emotionally intelligent individual can forge successful relationships and become an effective team player who is able to work cooperatively with others.

He can also use emotional intelligence to relieve stress, communicate effectively with others and relieve hostility or conflict. This is why emotional intelligence has been called people skills or social skills. Needless to say then that emotional intelligence is a very important leadership skill. In simpler terms, emotional intelligence is the ability to bring out the best in yourself and in others.

Features of Emotional Intelligence

Emotional intelligence embodies the following skills:

1. Self-awareness

2. Self-management

3. Social awareness

4. Relationship management

A person who has a combination of these skills can be said to have high levels of emotional intelligence. To understand emotional intelligence therefore, we must understand its features or the categories of emotional intelligence skills as listed above.

Self-Awareness

Self-awareness is the state of having thorough knowledge about yourself. Such knowledge when it comes to your emotional quotient has to do with thoroughly understanding your emotions. Your emotions are represented by your feelings so to be self-aware is to know what you feel at every given time. It is also to know what triggers which feelings and what actions which feelings lead to. Self-awareness is the ability to recognize each emotion as they happen. For instance, to know that you are 'getting angry'. It also involves knowing what point your emotion meets your thoughts and your actions.

Do you act immediately your anger starts? Or do you take in a good dose of the irritation before acting? Knowing exactly what point in your emotional curve you are propelled to act is a vital aspect of your self-awareness.

Your feelings trigger your brain to action, in a specific direction and this leads to your behavior. When you know in specific terms that listening to that rant a little while longer will lead you to tears, you can be said to be sufficiently self-aware. To develop self-awareness therefore, you have to tune in to your feelings. Some people call this your "true feelings".

You have to evaluate your emotions. You have to know when you are experiencing them. Sometimes, our bodies tell us what emotions we are experiencing. A widening of the eyeballs may signify surprise the same way blinking really fast signify excitement. Sometimes, I experience a rapid and excessive loss of weight, loss of hair and darker skin color that tells me I am going through stress caused by anxiety.

When I am scheduled to undertake a journey to a place I have never been, I go several nights with inability to sleep and that tells me I am anxious and uncertain. When I am afraid, I have temporary goose bumps on my arms and wrinkles on my forehead with my eyebrows pulled close together and my eyeballs widened. All these are pointers to the emotions I am feeling at each specific moment.

The same goes for everyone. If you develop your self-awareness, you might realize there are certain ways your body relates your emotions to you thereby reminding you that you are currently experiencing a particular feeling. Being self-aware therefore is having a knowledge of these signals and the emotions they accompany. This is the most vital part of becoming emotionally intelligent.

The major components of self-awareness are emotional awareness and self-confidence.

Emotional Awareness

This is the aspect of self-awareness that has to do with knowing your emotions. It is the ability to recognize your emotions and their resultant effects. For instance, knowing that anger causes you to cry, fear causes you to flee or happiness causes you to smile.

To develop emotional awareness, you must pause to reflect what you are feeling and recognize behavior that it propels over time so that you are then able to decide if you want this behavior or would rather avoid it by not allowing the unpleasant feeling to develop.

Self Confidence

To be self-confident is to have a healthy self-esteem, to be sure about your self-worth and your capabilities. It is a component of self-awareness because it involves a thorough knowledge of your strengths and weaknesses and your likes and dislikes and a belief in the accuracy of this knowledge.

Benefits of Self Awareness

Self-awareness portends the following advantages:

1. A knowledge of your strengths and weaknesses that enables you to work on yourself for maximum performance.

2. Confidence in your abilities.

3. Control over your emotions that enables you not to be ruled by your feelings.

4. Ability to understand other people's emotions as they occur.

Becoming self-aware

To become a more self-aware person, hold your emotions at the moment they occur and think about them. Of course, we do not mean hold them physically as emotions are intangible. Just take a deep breath, relax and close your eyes if possible and think about your feelings. Ask yourself 'how am I feeling?' and when you are able to recognize the feeling, ask yourself 'what is making me feel this way?'

If we practice self-awareness more regularly, we

would be able to notice when a situation is about to deteriorate and then walk away from it.

Self-Management

This has also been called self-regulation. It is that point in your emotional journey when you think before acting or speaking instead of the other way round which is the default way your emotional mind handles things.

During self-management, you transport your emotions to your rational mind before carrying out the actions they represent and indeed, you have the time to decide whether or not to perform those actions.

Self-management is the ability to control your emotions and your impulses and redirect them into more beneficial behavior. Although you cannot control the experience of these emotions, you can control the length of the experience or the outcome of the experience.

Self-management involves the practice of self-control, flexibility to change, accepting responsibility for your actions, trustworthiness, following through on your commitments, being open to new ideas and motivation. Emotionally intelligent people are highly self-motivated. They propel themselves to action by positively directing their emotions towards beneficial behavior.

Social Awareness

Emotionally intelligent people are empathetic. They understand the feelings of others; they relate people's responses to theirs and understand what those people are going through. By discerning other people's feelings, they are able to control their own reaction to the actions arising from those feelings. As a result, they are never quick to judge and they avoid stereotypes. They are good listeners and they focus on developing others.

Hence, they are service oriented and probably the most important feature of social awareness is that they understand how power works in a group. They understand the power dynamics in their organization.

Relationship Management

This is the feature of emotional intelligence that helps you relate well with others. You are able to influence and inspire them, communicate clearly with them, work cooperatively with them and defuse conflicts when they arise.

It is the state of being able to influence others as a result of having studied their impulses and responses under certain conditions or having experienced those impulses and responses yourself when you encountered those conditions and thereby knowing the most beneficial way to work or interact with them.

For instance, if you have been previously stuck in traffic for hours despite leaving home early and ended up with the emotions of frustration, anxiety and unhappiness, you will recognize these emotions in someone else when you see them go through a similar traffic situation and you will better understand how they feel and what their possible actions will be.

Someone who has gone through the loss of a loved one understands the emotions of sadness and grief when he sees it in another person who has just experienced such loss. He is much more able to empathize, to understand and help the other person go through his own feelings.

Negative use of your emotional intelligence in managing relationships is called manipulation and must be avoided by all means. The ability to manage relationships involve being able to guide your own emotions and therefore your behavior when in contact with others and also elicit the appropriate and mutually beneficial response from them. It is an essential quality of being an indispensable team player. Emotional intelligence helps you to direct your emotions and those of others in a way that ensures a positive relationship.

How important really is this concept to professional success? Has it now taken the place of or replaced technical ability? This is the scope of the next chapter.

CHAPTER TWO

EMOTIONAL INTELLIGENCE (EQ) AND GENERAL INTELLIGENCE (IQ)

We are now familiar with the fact that intelligence has been grouped into two: emotional intelligence and general intelligence although Howard Gardner, an American psychologist has posited that human intelligences were nine in number and everyone had an innate ability to develop multiple intelligences. Intelligence itself is difficult to define but refer to our ability to use our knowledge to affect our environment.

Emotional intelligence as we now know is the ability to develop thorough knowledge of our emotions and those of others and use that knowledge to direct behavior and relationships.

General intelligence on the other hand refers to intellectual ability, technical knowledge or cognitive ability. It is the intelligence that helps you succeed at school. It refers to an individual's capacity for learning. Both types of intelligence are used to predict success and we are constantly being assessed based on them.

EMOTIONAL INTELLIGENCE AND GENERAL INTELLIGENCE DIFFERENTIATED

A beautiful definition of emotional intelligence is that given by the psychology department of the University of New Hampshire as the "ability to validly reason with emotions and to use emotions to enhance thought".

Emotional intelligence therefore enhances your thinking. You get to reason out your emotions before carrying out their impulses. General intelligence, on the other hand, refers to our intellectual capacity and technical ability in our chosen field. It is also called intelligence quotient or regular intelligence.

Scientists have succeeded in creating a standard for measuring general intelligence in what is now called intelligence quotient (IQ) tests. These tests have now become a parameter for determining the intellectual capacity of a person. The test consists of a score derived after the individual performs a number of tasks evaluating his memory, numeric skills, reasoning and retention ability. A number is then derived to represent his intelligence. Creating a standard of measurement for emotional intelligence has not been as successful.

General intelligence has been used as an indicator of success. It has been applauded for a long time as the factor behind professional success but studies now show that although general intelligence is very important to high achievement, emotional intelligence plays a much bigger role in high achieving professionals.

This is not to say however that these two are opposing concepts. They are rather separate and work together to produce a perfect blend if both developed.

Differences between Emotional Intelligence and General Intelligence

We have provided six major differences between the two types of intelligence below:

1. As we have seen, the two behavioral models vary in their definitions. While emotional intelligence refers to emotional quotient (EQ), general intelligence refers to intelligence quotient (IQ).

Thus, while emotional intelligence refers to the proper direction of our emotions towards positive behavior, general intelligence refers to our capacity to learn, that is, our mental capability. Improving general intelligence will involve eating foods that enhance the brain but emotional intelligence is a different ball game altogether.

2. General intelligence plays a big role in academic success but emotional intelligence is more important for professional success. This is because general intelligence tests how a person can surmount new challenges usually academically but emotional intelligence points to how the same person surmounts problems in real life situations.

3. Emotional intelligence deals directly with relationships and helps you manage other people and your interactions with them, general intelligence does not deal with your relationships at all but with your tasks and how you can apply your knowledge to new skills.

4. Emotional intelligence translates to social acceptance. General intelligence has nothing to do with being sociable. In fact, people with high IQs

have tendencies of being antisocial where their EQ is low.

5. Emotional intelligence at work translates to teamwork, creativity, service orientation, initiative, motivation, achievement drive and leadership. General intelligence, on the other hand, is at play at work when staff members and management are able to translate technical knowledge to achieving results relevant to their field.

6. The challenges associated with emotional intelligence are social but the challenges associated with general intelligence are mental.

Levels of these forms of intelligence are varying between individuals and a low degree of any does not mean an individual is a failure compared to another individual. In the same vein, the fact that you have a low IQ does not necessarily mean you are not smart if your EQ is in place.

This is why John Mayer and Peter Salovey thought the smart politician was acting dumb. You can be intellectually gifted and not smart. This would mean that your IQ is high but your EQ is low.

Benefits of Emotional Intelligence

Why is emotional intelligence so necessary? Why do we even need to bother learning about it? We have tried to show so far that the emotionally intelligent people are the more successful ones. They are the ones who get help when they need it, are loved by everyone at work and are generally more fulfilled.

We would now classify the benefits of emotional

intelligence into the following heads:

1. Personal benefits of emotional intelligence

2. Organizational benefits of emotional intelligence

3. Emotional intelligence at school

4. Emotional intelligence in relationships

Personal Benefits of Emotional Intelligence

Emotional intelligence holds several benefits for the individual chiefly among which are self-confidence, creativity, fortitude, clarity and resilience. Emotionally intelligent people have a thorough knowledge of themselves and this increases their self-confidence and self-esteem. They are clear about the things that are important to them and they are more willing to speak for those things. They are not timid and they are able to set clear boundaries.

They are also more acceptable of change and able to withstand challenges that life presents to them. As a result, they bounce back easily from any adversity. Emotional intelligence also opens up their creative minds thereby making them exceptional individuals.

Emotional intelligence has been linked with physical and mental health. Emotionally intelligent people are able to manage stress easily thereby reducing their risk factors for some illnesses like high blood pressure and mental health problems like depression.

Organizational Benefits of Emotional Intelligence

An organization achieves its goals better with more emotionally intelligent people on its team, people who are confident, motivated, creative and personable. They also help the organization retain its clients because of their ability to build and maintain relationships. They navigate the power dynamics as well as social complexities at work more easily.

Emotional intelligence helps members of a team to overcome conflict by reaching a compromise. It also contributes to progress as these individuals are open to new ideas and enhances communication across the organization as team members are more receptive to feedback and try to see the good in criticism.

Emotional intelligence makes individuals solution-oriented and much more than individuals with only high general intelligence. Management can use emotional intelligence to inspire and motivate staff members.

Emotional Intelligence at School

The education sector in many countries are now keying into this behavioral model. School managements now use emotional intelligence skills to motivate their staff and inspire them to perform better. Students are now being taught in some countries how to use their emotional intelligence skills to perform better at school.

Although they need their general intelligence to get a grasp of what is being taught, they need emotional intelligence to help them get through their web of emotions and to relieve stress which is commonplace during examinations. A student who is 'preoccupied' with being bullied after school is much more prone to divided attention and lack of interest in the classroom than a student who is self-confident and able to coordinate his emotions and manage his relationships with other students.

In this way, emotional intelligence helps them to better organize their lives and their emotions around their studies. Students exposed to emotional intelligence skills have also been found to exhibit less risks of the antisocial behaviors associated with their ages such as drugs, pregnancy or violence.

Emotional Intelligence in Relationships

Emotional intelligence enhances relationships. One way it does this is by enabling the individuals involved to express their feelings more clearly, set boundaries and communicate them more effectively as well as draw into such virtues as empathy and mindfulness to support others.

By developing your emotional intelligence skills, you enjoy stronger relationships and then build a network of highly supportive individuals.

Superiority of Emotional Intelligence over General Intelligence

There are different opinions on this assertion. Some people think that general intelligence is more important and others opine that emotional intelligence is more important. But the perfect individual is the one who is able to build both of them. This is not an easy task and this is not to say that if you have low IQ and higher EQ levels, you cannot succeed. In fact, it is impossible to have such clear cut compartments of the two intelligences. We all just have a mixture of them.

More important however, is the fact that your

emotional intelligence level will pull you more easily through life. Your IQ will help you handle tasks at work effectively but it is your emotional intelligence that will help you keep the job.

CHAPTER THREE

ACHIEVING YOUR POTENTIAL THROUGH POSITIVE INTELLIGENCE

This book will not have achieved its purpose if we make no mention at all of the foundation upon which emotional intelligence rests. This is the concept of positive intelligence. Although emotional intelligence and the body of skills accompanying it as we have seen are basically matters of the heart and emanating from the emotional mind which is fully dedicated to our emotions, positive intelligence are matters of the mind and emanating from the rational mind.

It is a body of knowledge arising from the work of Shirzad Chamine and introduced in his book Positive Intelligence: Why Only 20% of Teams and

Individuals Achieve Their Potential and pointing to the fact that it was entirely possible to sabotage our efforts at becoming emotionally intelligent or intellectually intelligent through the negative use of the power of our mind. Positive intelligence is therefore a necessary skill for properly positioning our emotional intelligence. It is a concept bringing to our attention the fact that without solidly building the ability to direct our minds towards useful self-appraisal and self-encouragement, we may never achieve our emotional intelligence goals.

Understanding Positive Intelligence

Positive intelligence refers to the level of mastery you have over your mind. That is, how much you can control your mind to your best advantage. Your positive intelligence quotient refers to the ratio of time your mind serves you against the time it destroys you. Positive intelligence has three components as follows:

1. Saboteurs

2. Sage

3. PQ Brain Muscles

Saboteurs

These are thinking patterns that we have developed over a long period as a result of habit. They are the internal enemies that each of us harbor and that keep holding us back. They developed as a survival instinct but had become ingrained in us over time.

Although when we become adults we no longer have need of them and so they become of no use to us, yet we are unable to let them go because they have constituted themselves into our comfort zone. Their purpose is now extinct. As a result, they work against us all the time and make most of our efforts at getting better an absolute nullity. Shirzad has identified ten of these saboteurs as follows:

1. The Judge.

This is our inner critic that analyses every action we take mostly negatively and propel emotions such as anxiety, guilt, anger, disappointment. It is also the basis for all the other emotional saboteurs. It activates all the others and is a driver of negative self-appraisal.

2. The Stickler

This is the trait that is also known as perfectionism. The stickler seeks elusive perfection. It seeks perfection that it will never attain and by doing so creates an avoidable strain for not only self but also for others.

3. The Pleaser

This emotional saboteur accepts anything from everyone and cannot say no. He tries to please everyone and ends up a doormat.

4. The Hyper-Achiever

The hyper achiever evaluates himself based on what he has achieved and any self-esteem he has is directly proportional to his sense of achievement. He however never gets satisfied with his achievement because of the judge who pushes him to attain more heights in order to prove his achievement to himself.

5. The Victim

The victim is always seeking attention by being the person who is constantly trapped and who constantly needs help and he feels this way from inside him like the world is up against him.

The victim always reframes situations in such a way as to attract pity instead of looking for realistic ways out of them. His mind plays tactics on him to see why he must always need help and attention and why he can never stand alone.

6. The Hyper-Rational

This emotional saboteur has no room for feelings and thinks everything must be carefully thought out. In fact, it is intolerant of anything that is not logical and sees emotions as irrational.

7. The Hyper-Vigilant

He is trapped by the emotion of fear and is a constant worrier who is always alert to any perceived threats.

8. The Restless

This emotional saboteur keeps the individual constantly active and makes him feel like the world would come apart if there were no activity. He thinks that sitting down quietly and doing nothing is wrong.

9. The Controller

This one thinks it is his destiny to arrange things. Even when things go wrong, they could somehow be traced to him because he is always in control.

10. The Avoider

He constantly pushes responsibility away and never gets anything done. He even frames up polite ways to not do anything.

Sage

This is the state our mind is in when it accepts things just the way they are without judgment or criticism. It also consists of the ability to reframe bad circumstances in a positive light and bring out the good in them. The sage sees problems as either opportunities or gifts. The sage acts in the lines of the virtues of creativity, empathy and decision.

PQ Brain Muscles

Shirzad talks about two parts of our brains; the PQ brain and the survivor brain. The survivor brain is that in which the saboteurs live. As the name implies, it was developed in primitive times as coping mechanisms essential for survival but have now become extinct and of no use to us except to continually suggest self-limiting beliefs to us.

The PQ brain however refers to the part of the brain where the sage inhabits. It contains the middle prefrontal cortex, portions of the right brain, and the 'empathy circuitry'. It coordinates our positive intelligence by relating with our five senses.

This means that it can be activated using our physical senses. We do this by shifting our focus from the battle going on in our mind between the saboteurs and the sage to our physical sensations. In other words, the battle in our mind is expressed by our senses. Time and again throughout the day, check out how your thoughts are making your body react. Check out the flow of thoughts in your mind to any of your five senses and your PQ brain will be activated to deal with negative self-limiting patterns and beliefs.

These beliefs are recurrent but we must overcome them by constantly ignoring them and directing our energy towards self-uplifting thoughts. By activating your PQ brain muscles, you move from the saboteurs which act by default to the sage side of your mind which envelopes you in positivity and forge the atmosphere on which emotional intelligence could be enhanced and practiced.

Building your Positive Intelligence

It is important to know that positive intelligence is an acquired skill. It does not come to us by default.

This is because by its nature, our mind is more negativity oriented. We are much more likely to spot negativity and in fact we look for it in every situation. We are prone to see the reason we cannot succeed than the reason why we can. Sometimes we just think everything is up against us when actually they are not. To be positively intelligent, you must put in some work. You must develop your positive intelligence.

This is important because if you cultivate all the virtues of emotional intelligence and neglect this one thing, your mind will sabotage your efforts by your own self-limiting beliefs. By your personal belief that you can never be good enough no matter what you achieve. To build your positive intelligence therefore, you must do these three things; weaken your saboteur, strengthen your sage and strengthen your PQ brain muscles.

1. Weaken Your Saboteurs

You may or may not have all the types of saboteurs listed above. In fact, you may have a combination of one or two. All of us have the judge which recruits all the others to keep us in constant ridicule of ourselves and our achievement. We must identify which of the saboteurs we have and how they are limiting us before we begin to deal with them. We must identify the pattern that these saboteurs might have created. We must identify what they have made us believe about ourselves.

For example, is your saboteur constantly saying to you 'I am never going to make it?' Does it repeat it in a way that you now believe it? To weaken it, you must first identify it. Thus, you must become mindful. Remember that? Yes. It will be very handy here. Practice mindfulness and meditation.

Recognize your emotional saboteurs and acknowledge their presence. Don't try to shove them off. Saboteurs need your active engagement to survive. They need your participation. By practicing mindfulness instead of paying attention to the saboteurs themselves, you starve them.

2. Strengthen Your Sage

Your sage sees problems as opportunities. It believes that the solution to a problem is already wrapped in the problem itself. Thus, it believes not only in your ability to surmount it but also in your ability to conquer it. On the other hand, your saboteur sees problems as pitfalls that you may never get out from.

Depending on which one you feed the most, both of them are right. This is why it is important for you to shift your focus. Focus much more and if possible entirely on your sage. Try being nonjudgmental especially of yourself and release all criticisms. Accept situations for what they are. Always see the good in them and most importantly remember that nothing is permanent. Even terrible situations are temporary.

3. Strengthen Your PQ Brain Muscles

Exercise your PQ brain muscles. Think in a more positive light and generally create a more positive disposition about yourself. Use your PQ brain muscles to direct your mind to your sage. Use it to make your mind speak possibility and success into your life. Move your attention away from your mind to your senses and look back at what your mind has been telling you. Sometimes, the sage and the saboteurs speak at the same time and leave us to choose. We must choose that voice that propels us towards our full potential.

The voice that wins the battle in your mind is that which you choose. So capitalize on this and choose the voice of upliftment, the voice of your sage.

Achieving Your Potential Through Positive Intelligence

Our potential is limitless. It has become quite an axiom that our mind has unfathomable power to create our world. Hence, we have innate potential to be everything we want.

However, we are continually limited and held back

from achieving our full potential by ourselves; by the war going on in our minds. We are more prone to negativity given our primitive need for survival and so each and every time, we always see the reason why we cannot succeed. Positive intelligence posits that we should tap into the aspects of our minds that enable us to succeed. We should master our mind enough to compel it to work for us most of the time. We can do this by focusing and acting on the power of our mind to enhance our lives.

We should shift the energy of our minds from the negative to the positive. We should activate our PQ brain muscles. Experts have said that acting is what differentiates positive intelligence from positive thinking. If you must achieve your potential, you must not only make your mind think positive things, you must act your mind into focusing on them by activating your PQ brain muscles.

Remember that your thoughts create your future and so whatever you dwell on is what you experience. If your mind is continually judgmental of you, you will eventually believe you are no good and you will make no efforts towards improving your life.

CHAPTER FOUR

ENHANCING YOUR EMOTIONAL INTELLIGENCE

Emotional intelligence is best cultivated at childhood. This is done with the help of a parent, a guardian or a child caregiver who encourages the growth of emotional intelligence attributes such as thoughtfulness, mindfulness, empathy and care in the child.

Thus, people whose emotions were encouraged at childhood are more likely to be attuned to their emotions and how it affects others than people whose emotions were ignored. Emotional intelligence can also be cultivated in children by allowing them play games that enhance it. These games have been designed for this purpose.

It is a common thing therefore that children who do not play at all are less smart than those who do. They are also less sociable. However, emotional intelligence can be cultivated in adulthood. In fact, it can be learned at any time. This is the scope of this chapter.

Building Your Emotional Intelligence From the Inside

Whether you want to develop your emotional intelligence or you want to improve it, most of your effort will go into building the four emotional intelligence skills that we talked about in chapter one. You will have to develop your self-awareness, your self-management, your social awareness and your relationship management.

All the ways to do that are practical in nature. They involve a change in behavior that is conscious. They involve you paying attention. I have tried to categorize them and will explain them under these categories after which you will get to see some examples of how improving your emotional intelligence works in real life.

1. Managing Stress

The first step in your emotional intelligence enhancement journey is stress management. Stress keeps you from tuning in to your negative emotions and from practicing any of the things we have discussed in this book. When you are stressed and unable to manage it, you will not be able to identify the emotions at work; neither will you be able to think about them before acting on them.

More so, you would acutely avoid your negative emotions. This prevents you from experiencing them and becoming conversant with them. It is important therefore that you carve out a method to manage stressful situations. The most important thing when you are stressed is to remember to be calm and to detach as much as possible usually progressively from the source of the stress. Sometimes, this could even be people.

2. Mindfulness

Mindfulness is a very important tool for enhancing emotional intelligence. It is the ability to be emotionally present in the moment without judgment. To practice mindfulness, you must focus your attention on the emotions you are feeling and the signals they are sending into your environment including how they affect any interactions you might be having. You must also not judge your emotions. Allow them to manifest. That is like saying 'feel them'. This is so that you can recognize them. Do not suppress them.

Take notice of the emotional buildup of the person you are interacting with too before deciding whether or not to act on your own emotions. Here is an example. Mary is leaning on the dining table with her hip and hitting her foot on the floor while she speaks with Bernice.

Bernice is feeling her chest rise rapidly and this tells her she is getting angry. They are having a disagreement. Bernice notices Mary' posture and the dull tapping of her foot and decides not to say the words she was about to blot out because as she reasoned, it would only make the situation worse.

Mary is a good friend and fighting with her will only ruin their friendship by building up negative emotions. So, Bernice turns around and walks into her room. Mary is bewildered and goes to sit on the sofa. Not only is Bernice aware of her own emotional state, she perceives that of Mary as well and is able to decide on the proper action to take for positive interaction that would eventually save their relationship. Notice that all of these signals between them are nonverbal and neither of them have said a word.

We will consider this a little while later. Mindfulness posits that you be present in the world around you as much as in that inside you. Don't get too involved in yourself that you are unaware of how you are coming across to the other person; something their emotions will show you.

Don't get too inwardly oriented that you are unaware of the emotions flowing from others. This kind of attention will enable you decide appropriately and correctly what you ought to do next for the betterment of that relationship.

3. Emotional Insight

Emotional insight is your experience of your emotions and your knowledge of this experience. Developing it requires you to be mindful and observant of your feelings over a long period. It involves being able to know what activities trigger which emotions.

It is learning how your emotions work. It involves being able to answer questions such as how often you experience which emotions and in what situations. It also involves knowing whether there are any clues for understanding them.

Emotional insight is a complete knowledge of your own emotions after taking stock of your experiences with them. When you have a fully grown emotional insight, you know such details as which emotions you often experience and why, as well as which emotions you never experience.

Physical Sensations

Learn to listen to what your body is telling you. Our bodies often give us clues to our emotional experience. These clues could be physical sensations like goose bumps, a cold, a sore throat or even facial expressions like squeezing the nose in disgust or eyebrows lifting in surprise or distrust. You should know if you have a body experience that is linked with an emotional experience.

Personal Emotional Connection

Connect to your emotions per moment. Have a moment to moment experience of your emotions. Your emotions occur by the moment anyway but you should know that they are occurring. Also, emotions flow from one moment to another. You should be familiar with and aware of this flow.

Do you feel happy one moment and sad the next? Do you feel surprised one moment and disappointed the next? Improving your emotional intelligence requires you to have a clear understanding of this transitional experience.

Entangled Emotions

Emotions mix up with each other. Be aware of this possibility. You can experience two emotions together and be unable to actually say which one you are feeling. You can be sad and angry thereby merging sadness and anger together. Ask yourself, 'am I sad or angry?' 'Why is this making me sad?' 'Is this something to be angry about as well?' Learn to define your emotions properly and separate them when necessary. Tell yourself, 'although I am sad, I will not allow it to degenerate into anger'.

4. Develop fortitude

You should develop the ability to bounce back from adversity. Learn the lesson in bad situations and by doing so; you retrieve yourself from emotional doldrums. You are able to forge forward in spite of your challenges.

5. Reducing Negative Emotions

Well, like most things, when it comes to emotions, the negatives are the biggest problem. This is why I have found it pertinent to discuss them separately. Enhancing your emotional intelligence will involve dealing with them. So, you have to get to it. You will want to experience less of them and more of the positives. Reducing negative emotions involve two things; negative personalization and the fear of rejection.

Negative Personalization

We are all familiar with the phrases, 'you take things too personal,' or 'why are you taking it personal?' Well, yes. It is a problem. By negative personalization, you feel that another person's negative behavior is targeted at you.

You then develop negative emotions to deal with the situation, emotions such as anger- at their action or inaction- or emotion such as sadness. Sometimes and usually often, the behavior is not directed at us at all. If we are emotionally unintelligent, we would have acted before viewing the situation objectively. However, in order to enhance your emotional intelligence, you must either reframe the situation or create several alternative ways of viewing it before you react to it. For example, you may think your friend is avoiding a meeting you will be at because he is indebted to you whereas he is ill and unable to attend.

Thinking about the alternative possibilities makes you less prone to negative personalization. The bad situation or the bad response from the person you are interacting with might not be about you after all and most times, they are not.

Fear of Rejection

The emotion of fear, in this case, the fear of rejection

The fear of rejection can prevent us from attaining our potential or building relationships that matter to us. The fear of rejection is a strong factor for failure because you cannot have what you never tried to get and the fear of rejection is so strong that it keeps us from trying. To deal with this, you have to create alternative ways of achieving the same goal so that you gain comfort in the fact that there is another way of doing it. For example, instead of saying 'they are never going to like my product', try using 'I have advertised to five big companies, if one of them does not like my product, others might. At least one of them would contact me.'

Improving Your Relationships through Emotional Intelligence

Our relationships are our support system. At least,

some of them are. A vital road to success is being able to recognize harmful relationships and discarding them accordingly. Also, you must be able to categorize your relationships and know which ones build you up the most. But that is not the scope of this book. What we are concerned with here is how you can use your knowledge of emotions to make your relationships better.

To be truly successful, you must have strong relationships and a network of people to fall back on as well as to draw wisdom from. You cannot have any of that if you are emotionally unintelligent. So, how can you improve your relationships at work, at home, at school, in your career network by applying your emotional intelligence skills to them? How does this work in reality? Here is an outline of how to improve your relationships using your emotional intelligence.

1. Managing Stress

As we have pointed out, the ability to manage stress is the first step in the emotional intelligence enhancement journey because stress prevents you from tuning in to your emotions or creating the time to recognize or manage the emotions of others. What if the other person is the source of your stress? Let us say a boss at work or a difficult spouse? To manage stress in these situations, you will have to create boundaries and clearly express them.

Attach a consequence to the violation of your boundaries. The other person will immediately adjust to a position of respect. This also means that you do not bottle up negative emotions. Let the other person know exactly what they are doing that you do not like.

2. Mindfulness

Be mindful of your nonverbal interactions. Remember the story of Mary and Bernice? Bernice is able to decode the nonverbal messages that Mary is sending across to her. This is a vital skill of emotional intelligence. Practice mindfulness in your relationships.

Stay present in the moment and notice how your behavior is getting across to others and what their reactions are to it. When you are effectively able to understand the nonverbal communication in a group, you will be able to know the power dynamics of the group.

You will understand how members of the group relate with each other and what the unspoken rules are. This is a valuable tool for teamwork in an organization.

3. Empathy

You should practice empathy. Put yourself in the shoes of others before reacting to them. Show them compassion and show compassion to yourself too. Do not be judgmental. Do not be quick to conclude on others' behavior. By doing these, you will become a more considerate and socially acceptable person.

4. Managing Conflict

Emotional intelligence improves our relationships by helping us handle conflict appropriately.

Emotional intelligence teaches us to always seek the good out of criticism and ignore the bad aspects of it as well as discourage destructive criticism whenever possible by expressing our negative emotions whenever necessary.

For example, you can say to that person, 'I do not like that you spoke to me in that manner.' Always see conflict as an opportunity to strengthen your relationship but this is not to say that you should stick to toxic situations. When you are in a bad situation, be proactive rather than reactive.

Practice what your possible responses will be in such situations before they actually happen. Be slow to react to the source of your negative emotion so that you do not breed further negativity. Take a deep breath and refuse to respond.

5. Accountability

Be willing to be held responsible for your actions.

6. Responsiveness

Where the emotions flowing our way from another person such as a spouse are positive, we should learn to respond to them appropriately. This reinforces our relationships.

Practical Ways to Enhance Your Emotional Intelligence

1. Keep a journal of your feelings and emotions so that you are able to keep track of them.

2. Take a deep breath and close your eyes to relieve stress or before responding when you are in a bad situation.

3. Give helpful feedback and get it also on your actions.

4. Avoid manipulating others or being manipulated by them.

5. Pause to think before you act.

6. Think about your feelings. Take stock of them.

7. Always consider all the options before making a negative conclusion over a situation.

8. Be assertive whenever necessary.

9. Smile as much as possible.

10. Make your expectations of others realistic.

11. Practice listening.

12. Practice mindfulness.

CHAPTER FIVE

EMOTIONAL LITERACY AND ITS BENEFITS FOR SOCIETY

Emotional literacy is the body of knowledge embodying emotional intelligence. It refers to emotional education which speaks of deliberately inculcating emotional intelligence into teaching and the state of being enmeshed in such knowledge.

It has also been described as "the act of understanding, expressing and regulating emotions". Although the practice of emotional literacy remains rare, there are model schools who have inculcated these concepts into their curriculum for up to two decades with amazing results.

The problem with emotional literacy is the rate of

its spread. People who have inculcated it into their education system have seen a rapid change in the type of individuals the schools produce.

The programs have been designed to be both preventive and correctional. Thus, emotional literacy programs are often targeted at addressing specific societal problems such as drug abuse, teen pregnancy, violence or sexual assault. Emotional literacy is more effective if it is inculcated at an early stage and run all through the education phase of life.

It is also effective when parents and communities work together with schools to educate young ones on the subject. The features of emotional intelligence to be inculcated in the people undergoing emotional literacy courses differ by age and are best taught just before they start experiencing challenges that require those skills.

In their duty as correctional centers, schools teaching emotional intelligence are doing a lot of work curbing emotional deficiencies where they have already developed.

For example, some children were more prone to fighting and were unable to control their anger and their impulses before being introduced to the emotional literacy classes but experienced significant changes in behavior, in their approach to conflict and are more open to negotiation now that they take these subjects. As a result, they become balanced individuals fitting for the complexities of society and also much more beneficial to it.

Emotional literacy is also called self-science and the

courses teaching it involve subjects dealing with impulse control, anger management, conflict management, feelings identification, emotional vocabulary, self-motivation, recognition of the consequences of alternative choices and so on.

The results of emotional literacy are phenomenal when parents are involved in the process. The parents are then coached on emotional intelligence and how to become emotional mentors for their children.

They are also exposed to what their children have been learning in the emotional literacy classes. This way, the kids learn emotional intelligence both at school and at home and the lessons are consistent.

Emotional courses have been found to improve children's academic success and also reduce negative personal traits like self-centeredness. Emotional literacy does not stop at childhood. As we have pointed out at various points in this book, it can be inculcated at adulthood.

Everyone can become emotionally literate. We can all start by paying more attention. Teachers at schools offering emotional literacy have become more self-aware and have benefited from the courses they teach. Emotional literacy have been inculcated into them before passing it on to the children by management's insistence on positive self-talk, positive self-appraisal and better discipline options for violating students.

This has improved the mental wellbeing of the teachers themselves. Some schools have chosen not to create separate classes for emotional literacy but rather to introduce and merge it with the already existing subjects. Whatever the method, the important thing is that emotional intelligence becomes an early part of a child's training and remains until he is a fully grown individual and can continue his emotional awareness without outside help.

The benefits for society are enormous in that individuals are better able to fulfill their various roles to the betterment of all. Lives are also saved and enhanced by a teaching of emotional literacy. Teenagers and young adults who have a tendency for violence are better managed and sometimes entirely exempted by an early exposure to emotional literacy.

In the end, the society itself becomes a better place

to live in by a synergy of emotionally intelligent individuals who foster virtues of empathy, leadership, team building and conflict management. Emotional intelligence in schools make individuals more fit for the world.

Our lives and relationships are improving by knowledge of emotional intelligence and having that replicated in a large number of individuals will contribute immensely to the wellbeing of everyone involved and the pleasantness of society. It makes democracy itself possible. It is amazing then that emotional literacy is yet to be so widespread that every community practices it. What will be much more amazing is if we put in our own little efforts into making this possible. We can start from our homes with our own children making sure that their knowledge of their emotions and the potency of that knowledge is not left to experiments.

CONCLUSION

As I drop my pen, I recall my former boss again. Remember him? The guy from the introduction. His lack of emotional control has transitioned him to sitting in his office at his desk after a fitful outrage and begging the last employee to stay in spite of his ill treatment of everyone he encounters.

He explains profusely that he thought he was acting in their best interests and the suspension and dismissal letters were just a hoax and he had not expected the reactions he got for them. He had not envisaged that the employees would be happy to leave. He was concerned about being the sole proprietor who worked all alone and had no staff members. He was in a state of regret. The thing is, until you identify your lack of emotional control and deal with it, you will never get rid of your ability to continually build unhealthy relationships and to continually act impulsively, many times regrettably too.

There are lots of people in society. Some high achievers, others moderate achievers and others average people. What makes these people different? What is the factor for fulfillment? Is there one or more of these factors? More and more people are coming to realize that there is something which differentiates people and that most of it can be developed.

More and more people are keying into their emotional intelligence and their positive intelligence to achieve fulfillment. We have highlighted these important concepts in this book and we know that a careful practice of the principles embedded in this book will result in mind boggling achievement. We hope you experience it in your life.

References

1. Understanding the Importance of Emotional Literacy retrieved from www.pymblelc.nsw.edu.ay/blog

2. Five advantages of Emotional Intelligence in Business Life retrieved from www.eliteworldhotels.com

3. Thirteen Signs of High Emotional Intelligence by Justin Bariso retrieved from www.inc.com

4. The Benefits of Emotional Intelligence by Peter Taylor & Associates Inc. retrieved from www.pstaylor.com

5. How to Increase your Emotional Intelligence - 6 essentials by Preston Ni M.S.B.A retrieved from Psychology Today

6. Improving Emotional Intelligence retrieved from HelpGuide.Org

7. Emotional Intelligence and Intelligence Quotient retrieved from www.diffen.com

8. Emotional Intelligence retrieved from M.economictimes.com

9. Wikipedia

10. Emotional Intelligence: 10 Ways to Enhance Yours by Norman Rosenthal, M.D.

11. PsychCentral: Seven Ways to Improve Your Emotional Intelligence

'What is Emotional Intelligence?'

'How the four traits of Emotional Intelligence Affect your Life'

12. Dr. Daniel Goleman on the origins of Emotional Intelligence retrieved from sixseconds (The EQ Network)

13.Emotional Intelligence is more important than Cognitive Intelligence retrieved from https://ukessays.com/essays/ed

14. Positive Intelligence retrieved from www.positiveintelligence.com

15. 'What is Positive Intelligence?' retrieved from m.timesofindia.com/life-style/health-fitness.

16. Achieve Greater Success in Life with Positive Intelligence retrieved from theconsciouslife.com

17. Difference between EQ and IQ retrieved from ukessays.com/essays/psychology.

18. Emotional Intelligence: Why it Matters More

Than IQ by Dr. Daniel Goleman (1995, United States, Bantam Books).

47473879R00059

Made in the USA
Columbia, SC
01 January 2019